T0119621

SPEECH BEGINS AFTER DEATH

Michel Foucault, *Speech Begins after Death*. In Conversation with Claude Bonnefoy. Edited by Philippe Artières. Translated by Robert Bononno. University of Minnesota Press, Minneapolis and London.

Cet ouvrage a bénéficié du soutien des Programmes
d'aide à la publication de l'Institut Français.
This work, published as part of a program of aid for
publication, received support from the Institut Français.

Originally published in French as *Le beau danger: Entretien avec
Claude Bonnefoy*, by Michel Foucault. Copyright 2011 by
Éditions de l'École des Hautes Études en Sciences Sociales.

English translation copyright 2013 by Robert Bononno

Published by the University of Minnesota Press
111 Third Avenue South, Suite 290
Minneapolis, MN 55401-2520
http://www.upress.umn.edu

A Cataloging-in-Publication record is
available from the Library of Congress.

ISBN 978-0-8166-8322-2

Printed in the United States of America on acid-free paper

The University of Minnesota is an
equal-opportunity educator and employer.

22 21 20 19 18 17 16
10 9 8 7 6 5 4 3 2 1

Editor's Note

This interview was conducted in the spring and autumn of 1968 and was to be published in book form by Éditions Belfond. For some reason, the project was abandoned. We do not know how the text was prepared, but it is likely that Claude Bonnefoy is the author of the transcription. Errors and inaccuracies in the typed manuscript have been corrected.

We thank the Foucault family, Madame Bonnefoy, and Daniel Defert for their generosity.

Foucault and Audiography

PHILIPPE ARTIÈRES

In memory of Alain Crombecque

In considering the reception of Foucault's thought, several events have occurred that, to a lesser extent than in the case of Louis Althusser and the publication of *The Future Lasts a Long Time*,[1] have permanently altered the way in which we read Foucault and, more generally, respond to his ideas. For one thing, the publication in 1995 of the several volumes of *The Essential Works of Foucault 1954–1984*[2] revealed an oral Foucault. Now, readers had access to a complete collection of his statements, gathered from previous publications, which he had prepared for conferences, interviews, and other public events. This act of collecting, translating, and compiling contributed to the production of a figure largely unknown to many, forgotten or repressed by others—that of an engaged thinker, inventing forms of speech in public spaces, who was also an enduring critic of his own thought. Another Foucault had existed in parallel to the author: a man engaged in more ephemeral activities. The revelation of these two sides of the philosopher's activity was met with a particularly interesting response, namely, the specific notion of the intellectual (which many would claim began with Pierre Bourdieu) was updated.[3] Through the publication of roundtables and interviews, contemporary militants—those engaged in global social forums, for example, or concerned with issues of sexual identity—were given indirect access to the principal components of Foucault's thought.

The subsequent publication of his lectures at the Collège de France (1971–84) beginning in 1997, and their translation throughout the world, gradually doubled the Foucauldian corpus following the philosopher's death in 1984. Until then, those lectures had been circulated in the form of audiocassettes or unedited transcriptions; Foucault's teaching was misunderstood, ignored, or became the privilege of a handful of initiates who had little interest in sharing this work with outsiders. The publication of his lectures peremptorily disrupted this state of affairs. It provided access to anyone who did not attend his lectures, in fact, to any early-twenty-first-century reader, not only to an individual lecture or course but, with the completion of the publication, the entirety of his teaching as it developed. To the question "What does it mean to get involved?" was added a new question: "What does it mean to teach?"

Furthermore, this two-sided editorial event suddenly revealed the extraordinary range of speech registers mobilized by Foucault throughout his career and the strength of his investment in oral discourse. In other words, it not only shows the extent to which a speaking strategy existed for Foucault but also, and especially, reveals an ethical quest for speech, a search that was ongoing for him. The finest indication of this strategy is that he was able to turn the final subject he addressed as a teacher into a philosophical question, that of "speaking truthfully." His interview with the critic Claude Bonnefoy is part of this same matrix; shortly after *The Order of Things* was published, he began to experiment with language.

This practice of oral speech resembles what Claude Mauriac brilliantly chronicled in his journal, in which he incorporated phone and dinner conversations, dialogues, and meetings.[4] For Foucault, this practice was both unique and—as it was so often—highly controlled. The philosopher had incised a geography of his language gestures, one quite different from that of Jean-Paul Sartre,[5] Emmanuel Levinas, or Jacques Derrida. Not the kind of philosopher to stand on a barrel pointing out the road forward to workers, Foucault used speech in a way that, although it sometimes intersected practices characteristic of French intellectuals during the 1960s, shared, above all, in his specific activity as a philosopher. For Foucault, speaking meant possibly being inscribed within an order of discourse, but it was also a way of problematizing this practice through the gesture of speech itself. We can understand, then, why contemporary playwrights and actors have taken an interest in Foucault.[6] For him, speaking meant continuously reinventing a new theater, a profoundly political theater.

This geography of the voice, this "audiography," is composed of very different public speech acts that can be assigned a succinct typology according to their relative proportion. There is, first of all, the imposing mass of educational material (seminars, lectures, letters, conferences), the scientific and political discussions (roundtables, dialogues, interviews, conversations), presentations of various kinds (public gatherings, demonstrations, meetings, but not the kind of polemical exchange Foucault was emphatically opposed to), and finally the obligatory speech statements (inaugural addresses, oral exams, hearings before committees, invitations, cross-examinations).

This audiography is also associated with a number of physical locations. Some are institutional and expected—the university auditorium or radio studio—others are more incongruous. For example, the exchange on intellectuals and power took place in the kitchen of Gilles and Fanny Deleuze in Paris, and Foucault's discussion with Maurice Clavel occurred in Vézelay. He spoke on the streets of Nancy after the uprising at the Charles-III prison and in Paris, on the hilly streets of la Goutte d'Or. For the text presented here, Foucault met with Claude Bonnefoy, a literary critic with the journal *Arts*. The interviews took place over the course of several days during the summer–autumn of 1968. They were held, most likely, at Foucault's home on the Rue du Docteur-Finlay, before he had moved into the apartment on the Rue de Vaugirard, which he didn't purchase until his return from Tunisia. The first of those interviews—and the only one to survive—is published here.

This geography has left its imprint in the archives. There are bootleg recordings on magnetic tape (for example, his lectures in Brazil, Japan, and Canada, and, especially, his lectures at the Collège de France), texts prepared by Foucault (several interviews collected in *The Essential Works of Foucault*), a transcription of him speaking, notes taken by bystanders, often a student (Foucault was a teaching assistant at the École normale supérieure on the Rue d'Ulm), or, finally, a single photograph of Foucault speaking but forever silent—the celebrated picture of the philosopher on a street in the Goutte d'Or in 1971, a megaphone in his hand, surrounded by Claude Mauriac, Jean Genet, and André Glucksmann. Sometimes there is no record at all, speech has returned to silence, as in Bucharest in the 1960s or the Sorbonne in 1969.[7] What was Foucault saying that day before the crowd? No one knows any longer. From the archival point of view, the interview with Bonnefoy is of considerable interest. A typed manuscript of the interview is stored in the archives of the Association pour le Centre Michel Foucault. This transcription, most likely the work of Claude Bonnefoy, contains no corrections or additions by Foucault. The tapes have disappeared, the voices have been silenced. In 2004, for the twenty-year anniversary of

Foucault's death, over the course of two evenings, Radio-France broadcast a reading of the interview as part of the Atelier Foucault, which had been conceived with the help of Alain Crombecque and Daniel Defert. Éric Ruf of the Comédie française served as the voice of Foucault and Pierre Lamendé that of Bonnefoy. A recording of the reading was published by Gallimard that same year on CD. In a supplement to the daily newspaper *Le Monde* devoted to the Festival d'Automne, 2004, the first pages of this transcription were published along with photographs of the philosopher.

These very heterogeneous, often lapidary, archives describe a map that is not circumstantial but closely connected to the Foucauldian project. Within Foucault's intellectual development, it goes without saying that many of these language events are associated with the trajectory of his life and are part of a historical context that illuminates that same trajectory. In this light, we would do well to remember that the years bracketing 1968 represent an unusual moment of intense discourse by students and workers, as well as intellectuals.[8]

Two practices associated with this Foucauldian posture are exemplary: the press conference and the interview. Much could be said about the way in which Foucault, in some of his books, breaks the stream of univocal discourse by introducing a dialogue, as he does, for example, at the end of *The Archaeology of Knowledge*. But to do so we would have to analyze how he conducted his lectures at the Collège de France, gesturing, reading aloud from his sources—not without pleasure—or working on the radio monologues he prepared for France-Culture in the 1960s.[9] If we have focused on the interview and the press conference, it is because these two practices have clearly defined rules and help clarify the experiment undertaken with Claude Bonnefoy. Foucault did not invent these forms of speech, he subverted them.

The press conferences began a few years after the interview published here, during the years 1971–72, when Foucault worked with the Groupe Informations

Prisons (GIP). Embedded in this concern to turn information into a form of struggle, they take place in the repressive context of post-68 France, when the principal far-left political organizations were being dissolved by the government.[10] Foucault did not hide his concern, he went to the prisons to speak with the families and appeared with actors from the Théâtre du Soleil in sketches performed in front of housing projects on the outskirts of Paris. In doing so, Foucault engaged in speech practices that were novel for him. It was a question of using those practices to challenge philosophy.[11]

The press conference is not part of those experimental practices; the process is extremely codified and serves as a form of public speaking most often used by the power structure to orchestrate the transmission of its discourse. Journalists are convened to attend the press conference of a minister or president. This meeting, during which one or more publicly recognized individuals addresses those assembled to inform them of an event or a position, most often unfolds in two stages:

a statement by the speaker followed by a question-and-answer period. The physical equipment used is extremely standardized and resembles that used in educational settings. The speaker stands behind a desk or lectern, often raised, while the audience is seated. The power of speech is here doubled by a form of physical domination. It is precisely this mechanism that Foucault used during the years 1971–72, that is, at the time he obtained his chair at the Collège de France. The philosopher subverted this manifestation of the power of speech in at least three ways.

The first press conference in which he participated took place on February 8, 1971, in the company of Jean-Marie Domenach and Pierre Vidal-Naquet, when they announced the creation of the GIP. The group's manifesto was read and subsequently widely reproduced in the French press. The announcement was made during a press conference organized at the Chapelle Saint-Bernard, in the Gare Montparnasse railway station, by the lawyers for a group of imprisoned Maoist militants. Having struggled for weeks to obtain the status of political prisoners, they now announced that their demands had been met and their hunger strike ended. It was a form of victorious speech directed at the minister of justice, René Pleven, at a nonneutral location, a chapel, the site of another kind of power, that of religious speech. So, what did Foucault do? He attended the press conference not to appropriate or co-opt it, but to prolong it. He did not use it as an exhibition space, or a space in which to make a statement, but as an opportunity to draw attention. He stated that an investigation had been launched in the prisons to determine what had happened, who was there, and so on. To their victorious words he attached a questionnaire, to the exclamatory he added an interrogative. The press conference was thereby inverted, the speaker asked questions in place of the audience. The person speaking did not state any truth, he questioned the evidence.

The press conference that was held in a university auditorium a few months later, on June 21, 1971, was entirely different in kind. This time Foucault was not invited to the dais, he was among those assembled. The subject was what came to be known as the Jaubert Affair, after the name of a journalist for *Le Nouvel Observateur*, Alain Jaubert, who was badly beaten by the police after a demonstration in Paris by French West Indians in the spring of 1971 as he was trying to help an injured man who had not been in the march. Upon his release from custody, an unofficial commission was formed to find out what had happened. The minister of the interior claimed that Jaubert had attacked and insulted the police officers. Journalists from publications as different as *Le Figaro*, *Le Monde*, and *Le Nouvel Observateur*, lawyers and several intellectuals, including Foucault, participated. During the press conference of June 21, which followed one held a few weeks earlier at the home of Jacques Lacan and which announced the creation of the commission, there were four speakers: Claude Mauriac, Denis Langlois, an attorney for the Ligue des droits de l'Homme, Gilles Deleuze, and Michel Foucault. A brochure was published for the occasion and serves, aside from a handful of photographs, as the only record of the event. The speakers did not simply denounce a campaign of misinformation, they analyzed the way in which the power of speech was exercised through an official communiqué of the minister of the interior. With irony, and through a rigorous analysis of the text, the four men undid the mechanisms of this arbitrary use of speech. They countered it with the collective speech of the witnesses.

Approximately six months after the event, a series of uprisings shook prisons in France. They began at the Ney Prison in Toul in early December 1971, then spread to twenty French penal institutions; inmates mutinied and for several hours occupied the roofs of the prisons, yelling slogans denouncing the conditions inside. The prisoners talked about their situation, mobilized, wrote requests, publicized eyewitness accounts. They assumed the power of speech. An unannounced press conference organized by the GIP was held at the ministry of justice on the Place Vendôme in Paris during the late afternoon of February 17, 1972.

This became the setting for a new and unexpected event. Foucault spoke but read aloud from a text written by the inmates of Melun prison. In other words, in the very space were the law is decreed, the ministry of justice, the philosopher gave a voice to those who until then had been deprived of the power of speech. He did not speak on their behalf or for them, he served as a transmitter.

In interviews, Foucault again experimented with the exercise of speech. We know that following his return to France in the late 1960s, after a lengthy exile in Sweden, Poland, Germany, and Tunisia, Foucault had numerous requests for interviews in France and abroad.[12] Most often he accepted and explained his actions, his positions, his work in various journals and reviews. Yet, among those many interviews, four stand out, for they serve as genuine speech experiments, in which Foucault attempts to disengage from the position of power he occupied.

The interview that follows is the first. When Foucault completed *The Archaeology of Knowledge*, Claude

Bonnefoy suggested he publish a book of dialogues for Éditions Belfond. At the time, Foucault wanted to explain his way of working and agreed. But from the very first sessions, Bonnefoy framed the interviews in a way that made Foucault extremely reticent. Bonnefoy wanted to discuss the "wrong side of the carpet," to address Foucault's relationship to writing. Over the course of the ten meetings that took place, Foucault engaged in a new kind of speech, autobiographical speech. The author's intimate comments about himself led to an alteration in the oral exchanges between the two men, a modification of what had initially been a conventional interview. In discussing the way he worked, in expressing his difficulties as a *writer,* Foucault adopted a novel register, a new language. At the conclusion of the interviews, he said he had been transformed and was pleased to have succeeded in inventing a type of discourse that was neither a conversation nor a "kind of lyrical monologue."

Then, Gilles Deleuze, to whom the review *L'Arc* wanted to devote an issue in the early 1970s, suggested to Foucault that they have a discussion.[13] It was Foucault's only dialogue with a contemporary philosopher—if we exclude the debate with Noam Chomsky that took place on Dutch television, but which failed, turning into two parallel monologues. The dialogue with Deleuze is interesting because it is a genuine exercise in thinking. Deleuze and Foucault are thinking aloud, not about a text, not about a painting, but about their respective experiences with the GIP and during other actions. Although either of them could have articulated his work at the time of their intervention in the public space, together they defined, based on their experience, a new link between theory and practice. Their discussion is not a simple presentation of contrasting viewpoints, it results in a diagnosis of what was happening at that time; the interview evolves into a dialogue capable of producing new concepts.

Several years later, Foucault experimented with another type of interview, as reported by Claude Mauriac in *Mauriac et fils*, one related to the Platonic dialogue and which remains unknown to this day. Yet, those interviews did appear, in 1978, under the name Thierry Voeltzel, with a preface by that same Claude Mauriac.[14] But Foucault's name is absent: the philosopher is the one questioning Thierry Voeltzel about his personal experiences, as a young man of twenty in 1976, when the recording was made. Asking some very direct questions, Foucault engages in a dialogue with this young homosexual about his background, his activities, and his sexuality. Here, Foucault reversed the process; he became the questioner, and he found the experience to be extremely positive, for it resulted in speech "of great freedom."

No doubt the experience of anonymity should be compared with Foucault's decision in February 1980 when, after agreeing to Christian Delacampagne's request for an interview for *Le Monde,* he made it a condition that there be no mention of his name. Daniel Defert has indicated that the philosopher's identity during the interview, which appeared in the issue of April 6, 1980, would remain unknown until Foucault's death. By this gesture, which neutralized the effects of celebrity, he wished to avoid publicity and allow more room for the discussion of ideas. He was rebelling against the concealment of the author's thought by his name and the problems such a situation creates. Foucault, as he stated on several occasions, wrote so he would no longer have a face. Yet he found, by the late 1970s, that this goal had become impossible not only in his lectures at the Collège de France but during his various activities: his face had become that of an influential thinker. He became the victim of what he so often struggled against. Anonymity and the use of pseudonyms are one of the ways the philosopher can respond to celebrity. Thus, during the roundtable organized by the review *Esprit* on the struggles involving the prisons,[15] Foucault used the pseudonym "Louis Appert," after a nineteenth-century philanthropist by the name of Benjamin Nicolas Marie Appert, the author of a remarkable survey of French prisons in 1836. His desire to leave France followed from this. It was as if Foucault sought, through this pseudonymous interview, to rediscover something like a form of intact speech and the intensity he had experienced with Claude Bonnefoy nearly twelve years earlier.

For there should be little doubt, during this exchange between the philosopher and the critic, something completely original took place. It was a unique event: Foucault putting himself in danger.

NOTES

1. Louis Althusser, *The Future Lasts a Long Time* and *The Facts*, edited by Olivier Corpet and Yann Moulier Boutang, translated by Richard Veasey (London: Chatto & Windus, 1993).

2. Michel Foucault, *The Essential Works of Foucault 1954–1984*, edited by Paul Rabinow, translated by Robert Hurley and others: vol. 1, *Ethics: Subjectivity and Truth* (New York: New Press, 2006); vol. 2, *Aesthetics, Method, and Epistemology* (New York: New Press, 2006); vol. 3, *Power* (New York: New Press, 2001).

3. Foucault's influence on Bourdieu, in particular his political project "Raison d'agir," was pointed out by the sociologist himself on several occasions. See Pierre Bourdieu, "La philosophie, la science, l'engagement," in *L'infréquentable Michel*

Foucault: Renouveaux de la pensée critique, edited by Didier Eribon, Actes du colloque au Centre–Georges Pompidou, June 21–22, 2000 (Paris: EPEL, 2001), 189–94.

4. Claude Mauriac, *Le temps immobile, III: Et comme l'espérance est violente* (Paris: Gallimard, 1976).

5. Jeannette Colombel, "Contrepoints poetiques," *Critique* (August–September 1986): 471–72, and *Michel Foucault* (Paris: Odile Jacob, 1994).

6. For example, in 2009 the F71 collective was awarded Le prix Odéon-Télérama du meilleur spectacle by the Théâtre de l'Odéon for a play about Foucault and his political statements.

7. See *Michel Foucault, une journée particulière*, photographs by Élie Kagan, text by Alain Jaubert and Philippe Artières (Lyon: Ædelsa Éditions, 2004). See also http://www .michel-foucault-archives.org.

8. Michel de Certeau, *The Capture of Speech and Other Political Writings*, edited and with an introduction by Luce Girard, translated and with an afterword by Tom Conley (Minneapolis: University of Minnesota Press, 1998).

9. See, for example, *Utopie et hétérotopies*, edited by Daniel Defort, CD (Paris: INA, 2004).

10. Philippe Artieres, Laurent Quero, and Michelle Zancarini-Fournel, *Le Groupe d'information sur les prisons: Archives d'une lutte, 1970–1972* (Paris: Éditions de l'IMEC, 2003).

11. Francois Boullant, *Michel Foucault et les prisons* (Paris: PUF, 2003).

12. Philippe Artières, "Des espèces d'échafaudage," *La Revue des revues* (2001): 30.

13. "Intellectuals and Power," in *Language, Counter-Memory, Practice: Selected Essays and Interviews by Michel Foucault,* edited by Donald F. Bouchard (Ithaca, N.Y.: Cornell University Press, 1980).

14. Thierry Voeltzel, *Vingt ans et après* (Paris: Grasset, 1978).

15. "Luttes autour des prisons," *Toujours les prisons: Esprit* (November 1979): 102–11, reprinted in *Dits et écrits,* edited by Daniel Defert, François Ewald, and Jean Lagrange (Paris: Gallimard, 1995), 4 vols., text no. 273.

INTERVIEW BETWEEN

MICHEL FOUCAULT

AND CLAUDE BONNEFOY

1968

Claude Bonnefoy: During these interviews, Michel Foucault, I don't want to ask you to repeat differently what you've expressed so well in your books or comment on them one more time. I would prefer that these interviews position themselves, if not entirely, then to a great extent, on the margin of your books, that they provide a way for us to reveal the hidden pattern, their secret texture. What I'm principally interested in is your relationship to writing. But there is already something paradoxical about this. We're supposed to be talking, and I'm asking you about writing. But I have to ask a preliminary question before we start: how will you approach these interviews, which you were kind enough to agree to; rather, how do you conceive, before we even get into it, the interview genre itself?

Michel Foucault: I'll begin by saying that I have stage fright. At bottom, I don't really know why I'm apprehensive about these interviews, why I'm afraid of not being able to get through them. Upon further consideration, I wonder whether it's not because I'm an academic, I have access to a certain number of forms of speech, in some sense statutory. There are the things I write, which are intended for articles, for books, in any case, for discursive and explanatory texts. There is another form of statutory speech, which is associated with teaching: the fact of speaking before an audience, of trying to teach it something. Finally, another kind of statutory speech is that of the public talk, the conference we give in public or among our peers to try to explain our work, our research.

As for the interview genre, well, I admit I'm not familiar with it. I think that people who move more easily than I do in the world of speech, for whom the universe of speech is an unrestricted universe, without barriers, without preexisting institutions, without borders, without limits, are completely at ease with the interview format and don't dwell on the problem of knowing what it's about or what they're going to say. I imagine them as being permeated by language and that the presence of a microphone, the presence of a questioner, the presence of a future book made from the very words they're in the process of uttering doesn't impress them very much and that in this space of speech that is open to them, they feel completely free. Not me! And I wonder what sort of things I'm going to be able to say.

That's what we're going to find out together.

You said to me that, during these interviews, it wasn't a question of repeating what I've said elsewhere. I think I'd be strictly incapable of doing so. Yet, you're not asking me to share my secrets, or my life, or what I feel. We're both going to have to find a kind of linguistic register, a register of speech, exchange, communication that is not entirely that of the written work, or that of the explanatory process, or something told in confidence, for that matter. So let's try. You were speaking of my relationship to writing.

When we read *The History of Madness* or *Words and Things*, what strikes me is the presence of this extremely precise and

penetrating analytic thought supported by writing whose vibra-
tions aren't uniquely those of a philosopher but reveal a writer.
In commentaries on your work, we indeed find your ideas, your
concepts, your analyses, but it lacks this tremor that gives your
texts a greater dimension, an openness to a domain that is not
merely that of discursive writing but of literary writing. In reading
your work, one gets the impression that your thought is insepa-
rable from a formulation that is both rigorous and modulated, that
thought would be less accurate if the sentence hadn't also found
its cadence, if it hadn't been carried along and developed by that
cadence. So I'd like to know what the act of writing represents
for you.

I'd first like to clarify something. I'm not, personally,
very fascinated with the sacred side of writing. I know
that currently it is experienced that way by the major-
ity of those who devote themselves to literature or philosophy. What the West has no doubt learned since
Mallarmé is that writing has a sacred dimension, that
it is a kind of activity in itself, intransitive. Writing is
built on itself, not so much to say something, to show

something, or to teach something, but to be there. That writing is, at present, in some way the very monument of the being of language. In terms of my own lived experience, I have to admit that writing hasn't presented itself that way at all. I've always had an almost moral suspicion of writing.

Can you explain that, can you illustrate how you've approached writing? Once again, what interests me here is Michel Foucault when he's writing.

My answer may surprise you somewhat. I know how to conduct with myself—and I'm pleased to do so here with you—an exercise that is very different from what I've done with others. Whenever I've spoken about an author, I've always tried to ignore biographical factors and the social and cultural context, the field of knowledge in which the author was born and educated. I've always tried to approach what we would ordinarily call his psychology as an abstraction and treat him as a pure speaking subject.

Well, I'm going to take advantage of this opportunity by asking myself those questions and doing exactly the opposite with myself. I'm going to change my mind. I'm going to turn the sense of the discourse I had directed at others against myself. I'm going to try to tell you what writing has been for me throughout the course of my life. One of my most constant memories—certainly not the oldest, but the most stubborn—is of the difficulties I had in writing well. Writing well in the sense understood in primary school, that is, to produce very legible pages of writing. I believe—in fact I'm sure—that I was the one in my class and in my school who was the most illegible. That went on for a long time, until the first years of secondary education. In junior high school, I had so much trouble holding my pen the right way and tracing written signs correctly that I was made to do these special pages of writing.

So, that's a relationship to writing that's somewhat complicated, slightly overdetermined. But there's another memory, much more recent. This is the fact that at bottom, I've never taken writing very seriously, the act of writing. The desire to write took hold of me only when I was around thirty. Of course, I had been involved in what are called literary studies. But those literary studies—the habit of explicating a text, of writing papers, taking tests—you can well imagine that they in no way made me want to write. Quite the contrary.

In order to discover the possible pleasure of writing, I had to be out of the country. I was in Sweden at the time and forced to speak either Swedish, which I was very bad at, or English, which I speak with considerable difficulty. My poor knowledge of languages prevented me, for weeks on end, for months, and sometimes years, from expressing what I really wanted to say. I saw the words I wanted to speak become distorted, simplified, like small, derisive marionettes standing before me the moment I pronounced them.

Given this impossibility of using my own language, I noticed, first of all, that it had a thickness, a consistency, that it wasn't simply like the air we breathe, an absolutely imperceptible transparency, and then that it had its own laws, its corridors, its paths of facility, lines, slopes, coasts, asperities; in other words, it had a physiognomy and it formed a landscape where one could walk around and discover in the flow of words, around sentences, unexpectedly, points of view that hadn't appeared previously. In Sweden, where I was forced to speak a language that was foreign to me, I understood that I could inhabit my language, with its sudden, particular physiognomy, as the most secret but the most secure residence in that place without place that is the foreign country in which one finds oneself. Finally, the only real homeland, the only soil on which we can walk, the only house where we can stop and take shelter, is language, the one we learned from infancy. For me it was a question of reanimating that language, of constructing for myself a kind of small house of language where I would be the master and whose nooks and crannies I was familiar with. I think that's what made me want to write. Because the possibility of speaking had been denied me, I discovered the pleasure of writing. Between the pleasure of writing and the possibility of speaking, there exists a certain relationship of incompatibility. When it is no longer possible to speak, we discover the secret, difficult, somewhat dangerous charm of writing.

For a long time you said that writing didn't seem to you to be a serious activity. Why?

Yes. Before this interview, I didn't take writing very seriously. You could even say it was something rather frivolous. Writing was a waste of time. I'm wondering if it wasn't the system of values of my childhood that was being expressed in this depreciation of writing. I come from a medical family, one of those provincial medical families that provides, when compared to the somewhat placid life of a small town, a relatively accommodating or, as they say, progressive milieu. Nonetheless, the medical milieu in general, especially in the provinces, remains profoundly conservative. It still belongs to the nineteenth century. There's a fine sociological study to be done of the medical milieu in provincial France. We would find that, in the nineteenth century, medicine—specifically, the medical doctor—had become middle class. In the nineteenth century, the bourgeoisie found in medical science, in the concern with the body and health, a form of day-to-day rationalism. In that sense, we can say that medical rationalism was substituted for religious ethics. It was a nineteenth-century physician who said, rather profoundly, "In the nineteenth century, health has replaced salvation."

I believe that the figure of the doctor, as it was formed and somewhat sacralized in the nineteenth century, which took over from the priest, and gathered around itself and rationalized all the old beliefs and credulities of provincial life, the peasantry, the French petty bourgeoisie of the eighteenth and nineteenth centuries—I believe that this figure has remained fixed, immobile, unchanged since that time. I grew up in that milieu, where rationality is cloaked in a kind of magical prestige, a milieu whose values were contrasted to those of writing.

The physician—and especially the surgeon, I'm the son of a surgeon—isn't someone who speaks, he's someone who listens. He listens to other people's words, not because he takes them seriously, not to understand what they say, but to track down through them the signs of a serious disease, which is to say, a physical disease, an organic disease. The physician listens, but does so to cut through the speech of the other and reach the silent truth of the body. The physician doesn't speak, he acts, that is, he feels, he intervenes. The surgeon discovers the lesion in the sleeping body, opens the body and sews it back up again, he operates; all this is done in silence, the absolute reduction of words. The only words he utters are those few words of diagnosis and therapy. The physician speaks only to utter the truth, briefly, and prescribe medicine. He names and he orders, that's all. In that sense, it's extraordinarily rare for the physician to speak. No doubt it's this profound functional devaluation of speech in the old practice of clinical medicine that has weighed on me for so long and has meant that up until ten or twelve years ago, speech, for me, remained just so much hot air.

So, when you began to write, there was a reversal of your initial, disparaging conception of writing.

Obviously, the reversal came from further away. But, here, we'd get into an autobiography that's both too anecdotal and too banal for it to be interesting enough to dwell on. Let's say that after extensive work I finally gave that deeply devalued speech a certain value and a certain mode of existence. The problem that concerns me now—in fact, it has not stopped preoccupying me for ten years—is the following: in a culture such as ours, in a society, what do we mean by the existence of words, of writing, of discourse? It seemed to me that we had never attached much importance to the fact that, after all, speech exists. Speech isn't only a kind of transparent film through which we see things, not simply the mirror of what is and what we think. Speech has its own consistency, its own thickness and density, its way of functioning. The laws of speech exist the way economic laws exist. Speech exists the way a monument does, the way a technique does, the way a system of social relationships does, and so on.

It's this density characteristic of speech that I'm trying to interrogate. Naturally, this marks a complete conversion compared to what was for me the absolute devaluation of speech when I was a child. It seems to me—I think this is an illusion shared by all those who believe they've discovered something—that my contemporaries are victims of the same mirages as my childhood. They too believe, and too easily, as I once did, as my family once did, that speech, that language, doesn't add up to all that much in the end. I realize that linguists discovered that language was very important because it obeyed certain laws, but most of all they insisted on the structure of language, that is, on the structure of possible speech. But what I want to investigate is the mode of appearance of actual speech and how it functions, the things that are actually said. It involves an analysis of things said to the extent that they are things. The very opposite of what I thought when I was a child.

In spite of everything, and regardless of my conversion, I must have retained from my childhood, and even in my writing, a certain number of connections that we should be able to rediscover. For example, I'm greatly struck by the fact that my readers easily imagine that there's something aggressive about my writing. Personally, I don't experience it that way, absolutely not. I don't think I've ever really attacked anyone, not by name. For me, writing is an extremely gentle activity, hushed. I get the impression of velvet when I write. For me, the idea of a velvety writing is a familiar theme, at the limit of the affective and the perceptive, which continues to haunt my writing project, to guide my writing when I'm writing, and that allows me, at every moment, to choose the expressions I want to use. This velvetiness, as far as my writing is concerned, is a kind of normative impression. So, I'm very surprised to find that people find my writing to be dry and mordant. Upon reflection, I think they're right. I imagine that there's an old memory of the scalpel in my pen. Maybe, after all, I trace on the whiteness of the paper the same aggressive signs that my father traced on the bodies of others when he was operating? I've transformed the scalpel into a pen. I've gone from the efficacy of healing to the inefficacy of free speech; for the scar on the body I've substituted graffiti on paper; for the ineradicability of the scar I've substituted the perfectly eradicable and expungeable sign of writing. Maybe I should go further. For me the sheet of paper may be the body of the other.

What's certain, what I immediately experienced, when, around the age of thirty, I began to enjoy writing, was that this pleasure always communicated somewhat with the death of others, with death in general. This relationship between writing and death, I'm almost afraid to talk about it because I know that someone like Blanchot has said things about it that are much more essential, general, profound, decisive, than what I can say now. Here, I'm speaking of impressions that are like the back of the tapestry I'm trying to follow, and it seems that the other side of the tapestry is as logical and, after all, as well drawn—in any case, not more badly drawn—than the front that I show to others.

With you, I'd like to linger for a while on the back of the tapestry. I'd say that writing, for me, is associated with death, maybe essentially the death of others, but this doesn't mean that writing would be like killing others and carrying out against them, against their existence, a definitively lethal gesture that would hunt them from presence, that would open a sovereign and free space before me. Not at all. For me, writing means having to deal with the death of others, but it basically means having to deal with others to the extent that they're already dead. In one sense, I'm speaking over the corpse of the others. I have to admit that I'm postulating their death to some extent. In speaking about them, I'm in the situation of the anatomist who performs an autopsy. With my writing I survey the body of others, I incise it, I lift the integuments and skin, I try to find the organs and, in exposing the organs, reveal the site of the lesion, the seat of pain, that something that has characterized their life, their thought, and which, in its negativity, has finally organized everything they've been. The venomous heart of things and men is, at bottom, what I've always tried to expose. I also understand why people experience my writing as a form of aggression. They feel there is something in it that condemns them to death. In fact, I'm much more naive than that. I don't condemn them to death. I simply assume they're already dead. That's why I'm so surprised when I hear them cry out. I'm as astonished as the anatomist who becomes suddenly aware that the man on whom he was intending to demonstrate has woken up beneath his scalpel. Suddenly his eyes open, his mouth starts to scream, his body twists, and the anatomist expresses his shock: "Hey, he wasn't dead!" I think that's what happens when people criticize me or complain about my writing. It's always hard for me to respond to them, except by using an excuse, an excuse they might see as a mark of irony but which is really the expression of my astonishment: "Hey, they weren't dead!"

I'm wondering what the relationship to death might be for a writer like Genet. When he writes for the dead, when he wants to animate the theater of death, become the minister of that theater of shadow, he deliberately situates himself on the other side, the back of our world, both to attack it and to get beyond it. There's also a certain intent on his part to make crime attractive, to put the reader in the victim's place. His attitude is both poetic and passionate. In your work, it seems that this relationship is extremely different to the extent that your attitude toward death is clinical, neutral.

Yes, I don't claim to kill others with my writing. I only write on the basis of the others' already present death. It's because the others are dead that I can write as if their lives had, in a way, while they were around, as long as they smiled and spoke, prevented me from writing. At the same time, the only recognition my writing can afford them is the discovery of the truth of their life and their death, the unhealthy secret that explains their transition from life to death. This point of view about others, when their life has turned into death, is, at bottom, for me, the place where writing is possible.

Does this explain why most of your texts are about systems of knowledge and modes of speech in the past?

Yes, I think that, from that starting point, we should be able to explain certain things. And first of all the fact that, for me, it's always very difficult to speak of the present. Naturally, it seems to me that I could talk about the things that are quite close to us, but on condition that there exists, between those very close things and the moment in which I'm writing, an infinitesimal shift, a thin film through which death has entered. In any case, the topic we frequently find in all justifications of writing—that we write to bring something to life again, that we write to rediscover the secret of life, or to actualize this living speech that is simultaneously of men and, probably, of God—is deeply foreign to me. For me, speech begins after death and once that break has been established. For me, writing is a wandering after death and not a path to the source of life. It is in this sense that my language is profoundly anti-Christian, probably more so than the themes I continue to evoke.

In one sense, I'm probably interested in the past because of this. I'm not at all interested in the past to try to bring it back to life but because it's dead. There's no teleology of resurrection there, but rather the realization that the past is dead. Starting from that death, we can say absolutely serene things, completely analytic and anatomical, not directed toward a possible repetition or resurrection. And for that reason as well, nothing is of less interest to me than the desire to rediscover in the past the secret of origin.

For me, this leads to another problem. When I write, I couldn't tell you if I'm doing history or philosophy. I've often been asked what it meant to me to write what I wrote, what I spoke about, what I was trying to say, why one thing and not another, if I was a philosopher or a historian or a sociologist, and so on. I had a hard time answering. Had I been given as much latitude in responding as you're giving me today, I think I would have simply answered, quite frankly: I'm neither one nor the other, I'm a doctor, let's say I'm a diagnostician. I want to make a diagnosis and my work consists in revealing, through the incision of writing, something that might be the truth of what is dead. To that extent, the axis of my writing does not run from death to life or from life to death, but rather from death to truth and from truth to death. I think that the alternative to death isn't life but truth. What we have to rediscover through the whiteness and inertia of death isn't the lost shudder of life, it's the meticulous deployment of truth. In that sense I would call myself a diagnostician. But is diagnosis the work of the historian, of the philosopher, of someone involved in politics? I don't know. In any event, it involves an activity of language that is extremely profound for me. Ultimately, I don't write because I have something in mind, I don't write to show what I have already demonstrated and analyzed for myself. Writing consists essentially of doing something that allows me to discover something I hadn't seen initially. When I begin to write an essay or a book, or anything, I don't really know where it's going to lead or where it'll end up or what I'm going to show. I only discover what I have to show in the actual movement of writing, as if writing specifically meant diagnosing what I had wanted to say at the very moment I begin to write. I think that in this I'm being completely faithful to my heredity because, like my father and my grandparents, I want to offer a diagnosis. Only, unlike them—and it is in this sense that I distanced myself from them and turned against them—this diagnosis, I want to do it through writing, I want to do it with the part of speech that physicians ordinarily reduce to silence.

I apologize for invoking another crushing relationship. I think that my continued interest in Nietzsche, the fact that I've never been able to position him absolutely as an object we can talk about, that I've always tried to frame my writing in relation to this slightly timeless, important, paternal figure of Nietzsche, is very closely related to this: for Nietzsche, philosophy was above all else a diagnosis, it had to do with man to the extent that he was sick. For him, it was both a diagnosis and a kind of violent therapy for the diseases of culture.

There are two interrelated questions here that should help us to continue to analyze your approach. Isn't it to better control this diagnostic instrument, which in your case is writing, that the first books you wrote were about medicine or included it in their field of view? I'm thinking of *The History of Madness* and *The Birth of the Clinic*. In choosing those subjects—validated by their relation to the world of medicine—wasn't this a more or less conscious attempt to minimize your guilt as a writer?

From my current perspective, pursuing this quasi narrative, I think we need to strongly differentiate between what I was able to say about madness and what I was able to say about medicine.

If I return to my childhood stories, to that subterranean world of my writing, I strongly recall that in the medical environment in which I lived, not only madness but psychiatry had a very specific status, in truth, a highly pejorative status. Why? Because for a real physician, for a doctor who heals bodies, even more so for a surgeon who opens them up, it's obvious that madness is a bad disease. It's a disease that, overall, has no organic substrate or, in any case, none in which a good physician can recognize a specific organic substrate. To that extent, it's an illness that plays a trick on a real physician, that escapes normal truth, the pathological. As a result, it's a false illness and close to not being an illness at all. To reach this last conclusion—that madness is a disease that claims to be a disease but isn't—is only a small step. I'm not at all certain that, in the milieu in which I grew up, this step wasn't crossed rather easily in day-to-day conversation, or at least in the impression those conversations were able to leave on a child's mind.

If madness is a false illness, then what can we say about the physician who treats it and who believes that it's an illness? That physician, the psychiatrist, is of necessity a deluded physician, who is unable to recognize that the thing he's dealing with isn't a real illness, therefore, he's a bad doctor and, ultimately, a sham physician. From this—still in terms of the implicit significations that are inscribed more deeply than others in the mind of a child—follows the idea that madness is a sham illness cured by sham doctors. I think the good country doctor of the twentieth century, whose values go back to the middle of the preceding century, is even more estranged from madness and psychiatry than from philosophy and literature. By taking an interest in madness, I obviously enacted a two-part conversion because I took an interest in it and in the physicians who had treated it, but I didn't do so as a physician.

In fact, *The History of Madness* is something of an accident in my life. I wrote it when I hadn't yet discovered the pleasure of writing. I had simply agreed to write a short history of psychiatry for an author, a short text, quick and easy, that would have been about psychiatric knowledge, medicine, and doctors. But faced with the dearth of similar histories, I asked myself the following, slightly different question: what has been the mode of coexistence, of correlation and complicity, between psychiatry and the insane? How have madness and psychiatry been formed in parallel to one another, one against the other, opposite one another, one capturing the other? I feel that only someone who had, like me, a nearly hereditary suspicion, in any case one deeply embedded in my past when it came to psychiatry, could see this as a problem. On the contrary, I had never asked the question of how medicine in general and illness in general had been formed in relation to one another. I was too deeply, too insistently embedded in a medical milieu not to know that the physician is fully protected against disease and that the disease and the patient are, for the physician, objects that are always kept at a distance. I have a distinct memory that, when I was a child, none of us in the family could be sick: to be sick was something that happened to others, but not to us.

The idea that there could be a type of medicine like

psychiatry that isn't directly connected to its object, the idea that such a field of medicine might have been, from its origin, once it was possible, and in all its developments and branches, complicit with the illness it treats, and consequently with its object, is an idea that the traditional physician could easily have formulated. I think it's at the basis of this devaluation of madness and psychiatry by traditional medicine that I decided to describe both psychiatry and madness, in a kind of network of perpetual interaction. I know that several psychiatrists were quite shocked by my book, that they saw it as a mean-spirited attack on their field. Maybe that's true. And no doubt the devaluation I spoke of was the origin of *The History of Madness*. But, after all—and I apologize for choosing such an elevated example of such lofty patronage—we have known ever since Nietzsche that devaluation is an instrument of knowledge and that if we don't shake up the customary order of hierarchies of value, the secrets of knowledge run no risk of being revealed. So, it's possible that my contempt, this very archaic contempt, very infantile, and that further reflection quickly dissolved but could not entirely suppress, enabled me to discover a number of relations that I would otherwise probably have not seen. What strikes me now is that in the renewed questioning of their field by a number of psychiatrists, of psycho-pathological science, the psychiatric institution, the hospital, I find in many of them, better developed and argued, a number of topics I had encountered historically. They too, no doubt, felt obligated, from within their profession, to devalue, or in any case to dredge up and shake up a little, the system of values to which they had been accustomed and which the approach of their predecessors calmly relied on.

In *The Birth of the Clinic*, I assume you didn't encounter similar problems. You returned to the sources.

I said earlier that my medical heredity was present for me in the act of writing. In that respect, choosing medicine as a subject of study was something secondary and correlative. In *The Birth of the Clinic* it was specifically anatomy, autopsy, diagnosis, medical under-standing that was in question. But if this mode of med-ical knowledge has been my obsession, it's because it came from within the gesture of writing.

So, in writing about madness, on the contrary, the fact of writing and examining madness meant breaking with this mode of knowledge and taking a leap into the unknown. At the same time, your talent as a writer was revealed in your work on madness.

I couldn't tell you why writing and madness commu-nicated with one another for me. Most likely, what brought them together is their nonexistence, their non-being, the fact that they are sham activities, lacking consistency or foundation, like clouds that have no re-ality. But I'm sure there are other reasons as well. In any case, compared to the medical world in which I lived, I placed myself directly in a world of unreality, of appearances, of lies—you could almost call it a be-trayal of trust—by devoting myself to writing and speculating about mental illness and medicine. I think that given the guilt I felt about writing, in my stubbornness to extinguish that guilt by continuing to write, there was always an element of this.

I'm well aware that I shouldn't be telling you these things; rather, I want to tell you these things, but I'm not certain they're worth publishing. I'm a bit terrified at the idea that one day they'll be discovered.

Are you worried about revealing too much of the secret side, the nocturnal side of your work?

Does someone whose work is, overall and in spite of everything, historical, someone who claims to speak relatively objectively, who believes that his words have a certain relationship to truth, does he really have the right to talk this way about the history of his writing, to engage the truth he claims to access in this way, in a series of impressions, memories, experiences that are profoundly subjective? I understand that in doing so I'm undoing all the seriousness in which I've tried to wrap myself while writing. But what can I say? If I've willingly agreed to this type of interview, it was precisely to undo my customary language, to try to undo the threads, to present it in a way other than it's ordinarily presented. Is it worth the trouble to repeat in a simpler form what I've said elsewhere? It's harder for me, I think, but more interesting to return to its initial fragmentary state, its disorder, its somewhat impalpable flux, the language I've tried to control and present as a monument both voluminous and unbroken.

I'm pleased that you've accepted this adventure, that you've defined both the contours and the risks. To continue this exploration of the back of the tapestry, there's a question I'd like to ask. You've already discussed the heritage that produced the diagnostic attitude you apply to things and the reversal of that heritage, which you displayed by your interest in madness. But what's striking is that in your work, even when you speak of madness and medicine, writers who are neither physicians nor philosophers, and painters as well, continuously enter your work. The intuitions, the truths transmitted to us by the writers and painters you have chosen—I'm thinking of Sade, Roussel,

Artaud, Bataille, Bosch, Goya—appear to have been torn from a secret, mysterious domain that is limited to the domain of madness and death. In that sense, your interest in them seems entirely justified based on what you've just told me. But isn't there something more? Don't your frequent references to these writers and painters reveal a temptation for writing and artistic expression, an interrogation of their power? Isn't there something fascinating about writing that, by virtue of its self-reflexiveness, its self-investigation, its self-involvement, and its self-undoing, achieves a profound truth and in so doing threatens—threatens whoever employs it, whoever makes use of it—to give way to madness or death?

You've just formulated the question I've been asking myself for a long time. It's true that I've maintained a very continuous, very stubborn interest in the work of people like Roussel and Artaud, or Goya for that matter. But the way in which I question those works isn't entirely traditional. In general, the problem is the following: how is it that a man who is mentally ill or judged as such by society and by contemporary medicine, can write a work that immediately or years, decades, centuries later is recognized as a true work of art and one of the major works of literature or culture? In other words, the question becomes one of knowing how madness or mental illness can become creative.

That's not exactly my problem. I never ask myself about the nature of the illness that may have affected men like Raymond Roussel or Antonin Artaud. Nor am I asking about the expressive relationship that might exist between their work and their madness, or how through their work we recognize or rediscover the more or less traditional, more or less codified face of a specific mental illness. Finding out whether Raymond Roussel was an obsessive neurotic or a schizophrenic doesn't interest me. What interests me is the following problem: men like Roussel and Artaud write texts that, even when they gave them to someone to read, whether that person was a critic, or a doctor, or an ordinary reader, are immediately recognized as being related to mental illness. Moreover, they themselves established, at the level of their everyday experience, a very deep, ongoing relationship between their writing and their mental illness. Neither Roussel nor Artaud ever denied that their work evolved within them from a place that was also that of their uniqueness, their particularity, their symptom, their anxiety, and finally, their illness. What astonishes me, what I keep wondering about, is how is it that a work like this, which comes from an individual that society has classified—and consequently excluded—as ill, can function, and function in a way that's absolutely positive, within a culture? We may very well claim that Roussel's work wasn't recognized or invoke Rivière's reticence, discomfort, and refusal in the presence of Artaud's early poems; nonetheless, the work of Roussel and Artaud began to function positively within our culture very, very quickly. It immediately, or almost immediately, became part of our universe of speech. We see, then, that within a given culture, there's always a margin of tolerance for the suspicion that something that is medically treated with suspicion can play a role and assume an importance within our culture, within a culture. It's this positive function of the negative that has never ceased to interest me. I'm not asking about the problem of the relationship between the work and the illness, but the relationship of exclusion and inclusion: the exclusion of the individual, of his gestures, his behavior, his character, of what he is, and the very rapid, and ultimately rather straightforward, inclusion of his language.

Here, I'm entering a world that you can call whatever you want, the world of my hypotheses or my obsessions. I'd suggest the following: at a given time, in a given culture, given a certain type of discursive practice, speech and the rules of possibility are such that an individual can be psychologically and, in a way, anecdotally mad, but his language, which is indeed that of a madman—by virtue of the rules of speech at the time in question—can function positively. In other words, the position of madness is reserved and as if indicated at a certain point in the possible universe of speech at a given time. It is this possible place of madness, the function of madness in the universe of speech that I've tried to identify.

Let's take a concrete example. For Roussel, my

problem was as follows: what had to have been the state, the mode of operation, the internal system of regulation of literature for Roussel's incredibly naive and perfectly pathological exercises—the decomposition of words, the recomposition of syllables, his circular narratives, his fantastical tales, which he invented from a particular sentence that he worked over and whose sounds served as a guide, as a thread in composing new stories—to become part of literature? Not only become a part of the literature of the first half of the twentieth century, but play a very specific role, a very powerful role, even to the point of anticipating the literature of the second half of the twentieth century. Considering the positive function of the language of madness in a universe of speech and in a culture that excludes the insane, we can formulate the following hypothesis: shouldn't we dissociate the function of madness as prescribed and defined by literature or generally by the speech of a given time, from the madman himself? Ultimately, what difference does it make whether Roussel was mad or not, a schizophrenic or an obsessional neurotic? What difference does it make whether he was Roussel or not? What's interesting is that the system for regulating and transforming literature in the early twentieth century was such that exercises like his were able to assume a real, positive value, were able to function effectively as works of literature.

So, you see that my problem, which isn't at all a psychological problem but one that is much more abstract—and also much less interesting—is that of the position and function of the language of the insane within regular, normative language.

We've deviated a little from the initial problem and I'd like to return to it now, namely, your relationship to literature. I think we can do this by starting with the discrepancy that enabled you to clarify some of your research. A moment ago you were speaking of the naive, and extremely complicated, writing exercises that Raymond Roussel imposed on himself. Can't we see in the complexity of those exercises a kind of hypertrophy of the love of language, of the practice of writing for writing's sake that, in a

normal writer, one who is simply concerned with writing things that can be adequately conceptualized in a language that's elegant and efficient, would be referred to as the "pleasure of writing"? You yourself, at one point, spoke of your discovery of the "pleasure of writing." How can this pleasure manifest itself in a practice of writing whose goal is not primarily to become enchanted with itself, even if yours requires us to do so and, also, enchants us, but to bring forward, to reveal the truth, to be more of a diagnosis than a lyric song?

You're giving me a lot of problems with that question.

Maybe too many. We can break them down.

I'll try to answer the ones that seemed most salient. You spoke about the pleasure of writing and you took Roussel as an example. To me that seems like something of a special case. Just as Roussel magnified the micro-procedures of writing with an extremely powerful microscope—while reducing, in terms of his subject matter, the enormity of the world to absolutely

Lilliputian mechanisms—his own situation has magnified that of writing, the relationship of the writer to writing.

But we were talking about the pleasure of writing. Is writing really all that much fun? Roussel, in *How I Wrote Certain of My Books*, never stops reminding us of the struggle, the various trance states, the difficulty and anxiety that accompanied him in writing what he had to write; the only significant moments of happiness he talks about involve the enthusiasm, the illuminations he experienced once he'd finished his first book. Practically, except for this experience, which it seems to me is almost unique in his biography, everything else was one long, extraordinarily dark road, like a tunnel. The very fact that when he traveled, he drew the curtains in his compartment so he wouldn't see anyone, not even the landscape, because he was so consumed by his work, demonstrates that Roussel didn't write in a kind of enchanted state, one of astonishment, of a general welcoming of things and being.

Having said this, does the pleasure of writing exist?

I don't know. One thing I feel certain of is that there's a tremendous obligation to write. This obligation to write, I don't really know where it comes from. As long as we haven't started writing, it seems to be the most gratuitous, the most improbable thing, almost the most impossible, and one to which, in any case, we'll never feel bound. Then, at some point—is it the first page, the thousandth, the middle of the first book, or later? I have no idea—we realize that we're absolutely obligated to write. This obligation is revealed to you, indicated in various ways. For example, by the fact that we experience so much anxiety, so much tension if we haven't finished that little page of writing, as we do each day. By writing that page, you give yourself, you give to your existence, a form of absolution. That absolution is essential for the day's happiness. It's not the writing that's happy, it's the joy of existing that's attached to writing, which is slightly different. This is very paradoxical, very enigmatic, because how is it that the gesture—so vain, so fictive, so narcissistic, so self-involved—of sitting down at a table in the morning and covering a certain number of blank pages can have this effect of benediction for the remainder of the day? How is the reality of things—our concerns, hunger, desire, love, sexuality, work—transfigured because we did that in the morning, or because we were able to do it during the day? That's very enigmatic. For me, in any case, it's one of the ways the obligation to write is manifested.

This obligation is also indicated by something else. Ultimately, we always write not only to write the last book we will write, but, in some truly frenzied way— and this frenzy is present even in the most minimal gesture of writing—to write the last book in the world. In truth, what we write at the moment of writing, the final sentence of the work we're completing, is also the final sentence of the world, in that, afterward, there's nothing more to say. There's a paroxysmal intent to exhaust language in the most insignificant sentence. No doubt this is associated with the disequilibrium that exists between speech and language. Language is what we use to construct an absolutely infinite number of sentences and utterances. Speech, on the contrary, no matter how long or how diffuse, how supple, how atmospheric, how protoplasmic, how tethered to its future, is always finite, always limited. We can never reach the end of language through speech, no matter how long we imagine it to be. This inexhaustibility of language, which always holds speech in suspense in terms of a future that will never be completed, is another way of experiencing the obligation to write. We write to reach the end of language, to reach the end of any possible language, to finally encompass the empty infinity of language through the plenitude of speech.

Another reason why writing is different from speaking is that we write to hide our face, to bury ourselves in our own writing. We write so that the life around us, alongside us, outside, far from the sheet of paper, this life that's not very funny but tiresome and filled with worry, exposed to others, is absorbed in that small rectangle of paper before our eyes and which we control. Writing is a way of trying to evacuate, through the mysterious channels of pen and ink, the substance, not just of existence, but of the body, in those minuscule marks we make on paper. To be nothing more, in terms of life, than this dead and jabbering scribbling that we've put on the white sheet of paper is what we dream about when we write. But we never succeed in absorbing all that teeming life in the motionless swarm of letters. Life always goes on outside the sheet of paper, continues to proliferate, keeps going, and is never pinned down to that small rectangle; the heavy volume of the body never succeeds in spreading itself across the surface of the paper, we can never pass into that two-dimensional universe, that pure line of speech; we never succeed in becoming thin enough or adroit enough to be nothing more than the linearity of a text, and yet that's what we hope to achieve. So we keep trying, we continue to restrain ourselves, to take control of ourselves, to slip into the funnel of pen and ink, an infinite task, but the task to which we've dedicated ourselves. We would feel justified if we no longer existed except in that minuscule shudder, that infinitesimal scratching that grows still and becomes, between the tip of the pen and the white surface of the paper, the point, the fragile site, the immediately vanished moment when a stationary mark appears once and for all, definitively established, legible only for others and which has lost any possibility of being aware of itself. This type of suppression, of self-mortification in the transition to signs, is, I believe, what also gives writing its character of obligation. It's an obligation without pleasure, you see, but, after all, when escaping an obligation leads to anxiety, when breaking the law leaves you so apprehensive and in such great disarray, isn't obeying the law the greatest form of pleasure? To obey an obligation whose origin is unknown, and the source of whose authority over us is equally unknown, to obey that—certainly narcissistic—law that weighs down on you, that hangs over you wherever you are, that, I think, is the pleasure of writing.

I was wondering if you would clarify an idea that you sketched out previously in your concept of diagnostic writing. In the process of writing, isn't there another obligation for the writer,

that of discovering something, possibly discovering a truth he suspected but hadn't yet formulated? And in a similar vein, don't we always have the impression, when we write, that if we had written at a different time, the page, the book would have been different, would have taken a different turn, that the writing might have led us to the same thing, the same thing we anticipated, that we were looking for, that we had established as our goal, but by other paths, other sentences. Do you get the impression that you always dominate this method of writing or, at times, are being led by it?

That's why for me the obligation of writing isn't what one would ordinarily call the vocation of the writer. I strongly believe in the distinction, now quite well known, that Roland Barthes made between authors *[écrivains]* and writers *[écrivants]*. I'm not an author. First of all, I have no imagination. I'm completely uninventive. I've never even been able to conceive of something like the subject of a novel. Of course, at times, I've sometimes wanted to write short stories, almost in the journalistic sense of the term: to narrate micro-events, to talk about someone's life, but in five lines, ten lines, no more. So, I'm not an author. I place myself resolutely on the side of the writers, those for whom writing is transitive. By that I mean those for whom writing is intended to designate, to show, to manifest outside itself something that, without it, would have remained if not hidden at least invisible. For me, that's where, in spite of everything, the enchantment of writing lies.

I'm not an author because writing, the way I do it, the little bit of work I do every morning, isn't a moment that's been set on a pedestal and that remains upright through its own prestige. I don't get the impression at all, or even have the intention, of creating a body of work. I want to say things.

Nor am I an interpreter. By that I mean that I'm not trying to reveal things that have been deeply buried, hidden, forgotten for centuries or millennia, nor of discovering, behind what's been said by others, the secret they wished to hide. I'm not trying to discover another meaning that might be dissimulated in things or speech. No, I'm simply trying to make apparent what is very immediately present and at the same time invisible. My speech project is more farsighted. I'd like to reveal something that's too close to us for us to see, something right here, alongside us, but which we look through to see something else. To give density to this atmosphere that surrounds us and allows us to see things that are far away, to give density and thickness to what we don't experience as transparency, that's one of the projects, one of the topics that remains constant for me, always. Also, to try to surround, to draw, to point out that blind spot through which we speak and see, to grasp what makes it possible for us to see into the distance, to define the proximity around us that orients the general field of our gaze and our knowledge. To grasp that invisibility, that invisible of the too visible, that distancing of what is too close, that unknown familiarity is for me the important operation of my language and my speech.

Your books suggest analyses of past modes of knowledge or speech. That leaves us to assume that prior to their being written, there was considerable reading, confrontations, comparisons, choices, an initial development of the material. Is this something that was done before writing them or is it the writing that plays a determining role in the way you observe and sketch the landscape in which, for example, classical thought or the institution of psychiatry is revealed?

You're right to ask the question because I get the impression that I've been far too abstract. If you like, I enjoy . . . well, that's how I read, I enjoy reading, partly out of curiosity, in any case through a series of associations that there would be little point in explaining here, books on seventeenth-century botany, eighteenth-century grammar, political economy at the time of Ricardo, or Adam Smith. My problem—and for me, the task of writing—doesn't consist in rewriting those books in a vocabulary we're familiar with. Nor is it to try to discover what we commonly refer to as the imprecision of speech, to identify what it is in the very text of Ricardo, Adam Smith, Buffon, Linnaeus, that's in some way present—but hasn't been expressed —in the interstices, the lacunae, the internal contradictions. In reading those texts, I disrupt any sense of familiarity we might have with them, avoid the effects of recognition. I try to focus on their singularity, on their greatest foreignness, so that the distance that separates us from them becomes prominent, so that I can introduce my language, my speech, into that very distance, into that difference in which we find ourselves and that we are in relation to them. Conversely, my speech must be the place where that difference appears. In other words, when I take an interest in objects that are somewhat distant and heteroclite, what I want to expose isn't the secret beyond their reach, which they conceal by their manifest presence; rather, it's the atmosphere, the transparency that separates us from them and, at the same time, binds us to them and enables us to talk about them, but to talk about them as objects that aren't exactly our own thoughts, our own representations, our own knowledge. So, for me, the role of writing is essentially one of distancing and of measuring distance. To write is to position oneself in that distance that separates us from death and from what is dead. At the same time, this is where death unfolds in its truth, not in its hidden, secret truth, not in the truth of what it's been, but in the truth that separates us from it and means that we're not dead, that I'm not dead at the moment I'm writing about those dead things. For me, this is the relationship that writing needs to establish.

In that sense, I can say that I'm neither an author nor engaged in hermeneutics. If I were, I'd try to get behind the object I'm describing, behind the speech of the past, in order to discover its point of origin and the secret of its birth. If I were an author, I would speak only from the vantage point of my own language and in the enchantment of its existence today. I'm neither one nor the other; I'm in the distance between the speech of others and my own. And my speech is nothing other than the distance I assume, that I measure, that I welcome, between the speech of others and my own. In that sense, my speech doesn't exist, and that's why I have neither the intention nor the pretense of creating a body of work. I'm fully aware that I'm not creating a body of work. I'm the surveyor of those distances and my speech is merely the absolutely relative and precarious yardstick by which I measure that system of distancing and difference. In exercising my language, I'm measuring the difference with what we are not, and that's why I said to you earlier that writing means losing one's own face, one's own existence. I don't write to give my existence the solidity of a monument. I'm trying to absorb my own existence into the distance that separates it from death and, probably, by that same gesture, guides it toward death.

You were saying that you're not creating a body of work and you do a remarkable job of explaining why. But in response I would point out that your speech possesses a unique resonance today to the extent that not only does it allow us to mark the distance that separates us from past speech, and in doing so achieves its goal admirably, but it also illuminates the present, frees it of the

old shadows that weighed upon it. But that's not my question. When you say that you disappear into speech, it reminds me of another statement about disappearance that appears at the end of *The Order of Things*, the disappearance of man. After researching the makeup and development of the humanities, you show that at the very moment of their expansion, their triumph, their very fulfillment, mankind is in the process of disappearing, of being erased in the uninterrupted fabric of speech. Excuse me for asking what may seem like an impolite question, perhaps it's too personal and involves obvious similarities, but isn't there some relationship between those two disappearances—your own in writing and that of mankind?

You're right to bring up the question. If you like, we could discuss it during another interview or consign to oblivion the problem I tried to express very clearly at the end of *The Order of Things*. Certainly, between this theme of man's disappearance and my sense of the obligation to write, the work of writing, there's a relationship. I'm well aware of the risk I take in saying this, for I can already see before me the grotesque shadow of the psychiatrist, who will find in what I say the signs first of my schizophrenia, then of the delusional and therefore nonobjective, untrue, irrational, unscientific nature of what I've said in my books.

I know I'm taking this risk, but I do so with absolutely no second thoughts. These interviews, which you were kind enough to request, have been so enjoyable for me because I'm not trying to use them to explain myself better and at greater length about what I've said in my books. I don't think that would be possible during these interviews, especially in this room, which I feel is already populated with thousands of copies of the future book, thousands of faces that will read it, where this third presence—the book and its future readers—is extraordinarily weighty. I'm very pleased that we don't know where we're going. What we're doing here is a kind of experiment. I'm trying to delineate for the first time, in the first person, this neutral, objective discourse in which I've never stopped trying to erase myself when I write my books. Consequently, the relationship you mentioned between the disappearance of man and my experience of writing is obvious. People will make of that what they will. No doubt, they'll criticize the chimerical nature of what I've wanted to assert. Maybe others will find that what I'm telling you isn't really sincere, but a projection of the more or less theoretical and ideological themes I've tried to formulate in my books. It doesn't really matter how they read this relationship or the book's connection to me or mine to the book. In any case, I know that my books will be compromised by what I say, and me as well. So, let's show that relationship, let's show that communication.

How do you experience the activity of writing, this disappearance in writing at the moment of writing?

When I write, I always have something in mind. At the same time, I always address something that's outside myself, an object, a domain that can be described, grammar or seventeenth-century political economy, or the experience of madness throughout the classical period. And yet, that object, that domain, I don't get the impression that I'm describing it at all, of placing myself in a position of receptivity to what it says, of translating with words on paper and with a certain style a certain representation I've created of what I'm trying to describe. Earlier, I said that I'm trying to reveal the distance I have, that we have to these things; my writing is the discovery of that distance. I'd add that, in one sense, my head is empty when I begin to write, even though my mind is always directed toward a specific object. Obviously, that means that, for me, writing is an exhausting activity, very difficult, filled with anxiety. I'm always afraid of messing up; naturally, I mess up, I fail all the time. This means that what encourages me to write isn't so much the discovery or certainty of a certain relationship, of a certain truth, but rather the feeling I have of a certain kind of writing, a certain mode of operation of my writing, a certain style that will bring that distance into focus.

For example, one day in Madrid, I had been fascinated by Velázquez's *Las Meninas*. I'd been looking at the painting for a long time, just like that, without thinking about talking about it someday, much less of describing it—which at the time would have seemed derisive and ridiculous. And then one day, I don't recall how, without having looked at it since, without even having looked at a reproduction, I had this urge to write about the painting from memory, to describe what was in it. As soon as I tried to describe it, a certain coloration of language, a certain rhythm, a certain form of analysis, especially, gave me the impression, the near certainty—false, perhaps—that I had found exactly the right language by which the distance between ourselves and the classical philosophy of representation and classical ideas of order and resemblance could come into focus and be evaluated. That's how I began to write *The Order of Things*. For that book I used material I had gathered in the preceding years almost at random, without knowing what I would do with it, with no certainty about the possibility of ever writing an essay. In a way it was like examining a kind of inert material, an abandoned garden of some sort, an unusable expanse, which I surveyed the way I imagine the sculptor of old, the sculptor of the seventeenth or eighteenth century, might contemplate, might touch the block of marble he didn't yet know what to do with.

[*The transcript breaks off here.*]

CHRONOLOGIES OF MICHEL FOUCAULT
AND CLAUDE BONNEFOY

MICHEL FOUCAULT (1926–1984)

1926: Born in Poitiers, France

1946: Enters the École Normale Supérieure. Studies philosophy and psychology.

1957: Is sent to Sweden, Poland, and Germany by the Ministry of Foreign Affairs.

1961: *History of Madness*

1963: *The Birth of the Clinic*

1966: *The Order of Things*

1968: Interviews with Claude Bonnefoy

1969: *The Archaeology of Knowledge*

1970: Appointed professor at Collège de France

1971–72: Works with Groupe d'Information sur les Prisons (GIP), which he founded with Pierre Vidal-Naquet and Jean-Marie Domenach.

1976–84: *The History of Sexuality* (three volumes)

1984: Died in Paris

1995: *The Essential Works of Foucault, 1954–1984* (Volume 1, *Ethics: Subjectivity and Truth;* Volume 2, *Aesthetics, Method, and Epistemology;* Volume 3, *Power*).

1997: Initial publication of his lectures at Collège de France

CLAUDE BONNEFOY (1929–1979)

1929: Born in Clermont-Ferrand, France

1948: Paul Valéry prize for poetry

1964: Literary critic for *Arts,* then for *Nouvel Observateur* and *La Quinzaine littéraire*

1966: Interviews with Eugène Ionesco; republished in 1977 as *Entre la vie et le rêve.*

1968: Interviews with Michel Foucault

1975: *La poésie française des origines à nos jours* (anthology)

MICHEL FOUCAULT (1926–1984) was a French historian and philosopher associated with the structuralist and poststructuralist movements. He is often considered the most influential social theorist of the second half of the twentieth century, not only in philosophy but in a wide range of disciplines in the humanities and social sciences. Among his most notable books are *Madness and Civilization*, *Discipline and Punish*, and *The History of Sexuality*.

PHILIPPE ARTIÈRES is a French historian at Le Centre national de la recherche scientifique in Paris. He is president of Centre Michel Foucault.

ROBERT BONONNO is a translator based in New York City. His translations include *Cosmopolitics I and II* by Isabelle Stengers (Minnesota, 2010 and 2011) and *The Singular Objects of Architecture* by Jean Baudrillard and Jean Nouvel (Minnesota, 2005).